Timeless Wisdom

Thoughts on life. . .the way it should be.

Compiled by Gary W. Fenchuk

©1994, 2nd printing 1995
by Cake Eaters, Inc. All rights reserved.
Printed by Cadmus Promotional Print Division
Richmond, VA

Cake Eaters
P. O. Box 1
Midlothian, VA
(804) 739-3

D1009197

Any suggestions, questio
or criticism are we

To Christy and Jason,
who have helped me understand
the real essence of life:
Love is central;
people, not things, are important;
and the moment is now.

and

To Mom,
*"What the mother sings
to the cradle goes all
the way down to the coffin."*

Henry Ward Beecher

With deepest love and respect, thank you
for being such a
perfect role model.

(Sorry it didn't all stick. . .)

Introduction

Ever since my college days, I have been an avid student of philosophy and quotations. Like so many others, I embarked on a futile search for the Meaning of Life. During this thirty year quest I consulted hundreds of books and thousands upon thousands of thoughts and quotations.

Well, alas...I, of course, have **not** discovered The Answer. And, in fact, I have concluded that there is no single answer or panacea—at least not for me. Life seems to be far too complex and mysterious for that to be the case. However, what I have discovered along the way are some universal truths and eternal values—all of which I have embraced as partial answers as I struggled to forge my own coherent personal philosophy/religion.

During my search, I developed a growing frustration with the inadequacy of quotation books. Virtually all of them seemed to fall within two undesirable categories— they were either voluminous reference books which were no more than dictionaries of thoughts (interesting to only the most desperate of students, such as myself) or "cookie-cutter" publications offering a collection of indiscriminate selections of superficial, humdrum platitudes. It astounded me that no one had successfully published a discerning collection of the best thoughts of mankind. I felt sure that many others, like myself, were eagerly seeking the ultimate book filled with relevant, profound, provocative insights which could make a true impact on one's life. And as my exhaustive, endless search continued, I silently vowed to some day compile such a book...

So block out an hour alone, get comfortable in your favorite spot and experience the exhilaration of ruminating with the Masters on this crazy thing called Life.

Acknowledgements

Quotation books have become a dime a dozen of late. Unfortunately, these publications have been more characterized by their quantity rather than their quality.

With this in mind, there has been a concerted effort to make certain that *Timeless Wisdom* did not become just another mediocre collection of "personal favorites". In order to assure that *Timeless Wisdom* enjoys more universal appeal, I have employed a unique concept of vigorous market-testing. This process was accomplished through a selective group of individuals who have been dubbed "The Committee of Twenty-five". These participants expended countless hours in assessing and ranking a multitude of prospective quotations. Unquestionably, the insightful feedback from this group served to temper my own highly fallible judgment and helped distill these thoughts into the best quotation book ever published.

I am extremely indebted to these individuals and wish to acknowledge their crucial contribution. The committee was comprised of:

Mike Beato, J. B. and Lois Campbell, Tom Carr, Bob and Linda Cary, Roland Diaz, Brenda Etheridge, Dorothy Fenchuk, Patti Fenchuk, Mark and Karen Fredrichs, Jo Frierson, Robbie Rice, Pat Hegdal, Eric and Judy Johnson, Jim and Pat Kracht, Liz Paul, Kathy Pearson, Roger Perry, Franny Powell, Louise Robinson, Bob Russell, Bette Schmidt, Roy and Barbara Sutton, Linda Tincher, Nan Walters and Catherine Weill

In particular, I would like to recognize and thank two individuals for their extraordinary commitment and dedication to this undertaking. Pat Hegdal, a long-time friend, and Mike Beato, my brother-in-law, contributed endless hours of wisdom and expertise and effectively served as co-editors on this publication.

Additionally, it is imperative to cite the behind-the-scenes, but highly creative efforts of four individuals, Connie Pollard, Debbie Gordon, Liz Heuple and Nan Walters, who helped convert an unorganized mountain of notecards into a highly professional and marketable product.

And last, but not least, I would like to acknowledge the ultimate contribution of my wife, Patti, who has had to endure twenty-three years of living with a frustrated philosopher. Through it all, she amazingly has managed to remain loving, encouraging and supportive.

Table of Contents

Men stumble over the truth from time to time, but most pick themselves up and hurry off as if nothing happened.

Sir Winston Churchill (1874–1965)

Nothing in life is more exciting and rewarding than the sudden flash of insight that leaves you a changed person—not only changed, but for the better.

Arthur Gordon

Man's mind, stretched to a new idea, never goes back to its original dimensions.

Oliver Wendell Holmes

The books that help you most, are those which make you think the most.

Theodore Parker (1810–60)

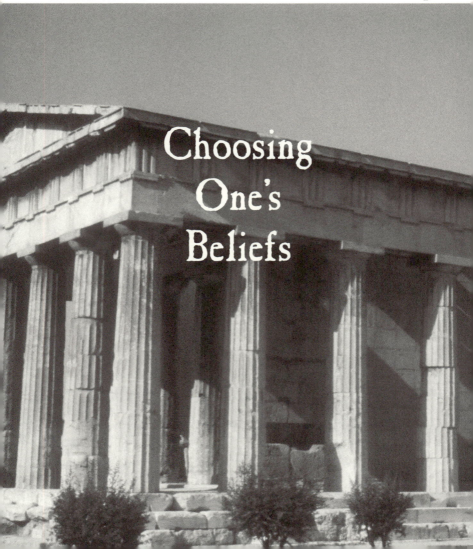

Choosing One's Beliefs

The life which is unexamined is not worth living.

Plato (427–347 B.C.)

All men should strive to learn before they die—what they are running from, and to, and why.

James Thurber (1894–1961)

Everything has been figured out except how to live.

Jean-Paul Sartre (1905–80)

Every man is a creature of the age in which he lives, very few are able to raise themselves above the ideas of the time.

Voltaire (1694–1778)

We are all tattooed in our cradles with the beliefs of our tribe. You cannot educate a man wholly out of the superstitious fears which were implanted in his imagination, no matter how utterly his reason may reject them.

Oliver Wendell Holmes, Sr. (1809–94)

We live in a world of many illusions and much of human belief and behavior is ritualized nonsense.

Wes "Scoop" Nisker

Perhaps in time the so-called Dark Ages will be thought of as including our own.

G. C. Lichtenberg (1742–99)

A great-souled hero must transcend the slavish thinking of those around him.

Friedrich Nietzsche (1844–1900)

Perhaps it would be a good idea, fantastic as it sounds, to muffle every telephone, stop every motor and halt all activity for an hour some day to give people a chance to ponder for a few minutes on **what it is all about, why they are living and what they really want.**

James Truslow Adams (1878–1949)

Why not spend some time in determining what is worthwhile for **us**, and then go after that?

William Ross

No man is free who is not master of himself.

Epictetus (60–110 A.D.)

Poor is the man whose pleasures depend upon the permission of another.

Madonna

Live 20% outside the "proper" zone; remember that the great wise men of the past held no respect for today's conventions, and neither will the great men of the future.

G.W.F.

Selfishness is not living as one wishes to live, it is asking others to live as one wishes to live.

Oscar Wilde (1854–1900)

The hardest fight a man has to fight is to live in a world where every single day someone is trying to make you someone you do not want to be.

e.e. cummings (1894–1962)

Before his death, Rabbi Zyusa said, "In the coming world, they will not ask me: 'Why were you not Moses?' They will ask me: 'Why were you not Zyusa?'"

Martin Buber (1878–1965)

Do not let your peace depend on the hearts of men; whatever they say about you, good or bad, you are not because of it another man—for as you are, you are.

Thomas à Kempis (1380–1471)

What you think of yourself is much more important than what others think of you.

Seneca (4 B.C.–65 A.D.)

I cannot give you the formula for success, but I can give you the formula for failure— try to please everybody.

Herbert Bayard Swope (1882–1958)

The truly great consider first, how they may gain the approbation of God; and secondly, that of their own conscience; **having done this**, they would then willingly conciliate the good opinion of their fellowmen.

Caleb Charles Colton (1780–1832)

Do well and right and let the world sink.

Author Unknown

Great tranquility of heart is his who cares for neither praise nor blame.

Thomas à Kempis (1380–1471)

He who seeks only for applause from without has all his happiness in another's keeping.

Oliver Goldsmith (1728–74)

Either control your own destiny, or someone else will!

John F. Welch, Jr.

The happiness of your life depends upon
the quality of your thoughts.

Marcus Antonius (86–161 A.D.)

We create our fortune, for so the universe
was wrought. **Thought is another name for
fate**; choose then your destiny and wait, for
love brings love, and hate brings hate.

Van Dyke

The soul becomes dyed with the color of
its thoughts.

Marcus Aurelius (120–180 A.D.)

The game of life is the game of boomerangs. Our thoughts, deeds and words return to us sooner or later, with astounding accuracy.

Florence Shinn

A thought (good or evil), an act, in time a habit—so runs life's law.

Ralph Waldo Trine

Watch your thoughts; they become words. Watch your words; they become actions. Watch your actions; they become habits. Watch your habits; they become character. Watch your character; it becomes your destiny.

Frank Outlaw

Watch your **beliefs**; they control your thoughts.

G.W.F.

A belief is not merely an idea that the mind possesses; it is an idea that possesses the mind.

Robert Bolton

The most powerful thing you can do to change the world is to **change your own beliefs** about the nature of life, people and reality to something more positive...**and begin to act accordingly.**

Shakti Gawain

The most important thing about a man is his view of the universe.

G. K. Chesterton (1874–1936)

As we think in our hearts, so we are.

Proverbs 23:7

All that we are is the result of what we have thought. The mind is everything. What we think, we become.

Buddha (563–483 B.C.)

Rule your mind or it will rule you.

Horace (65–8 B.C.)

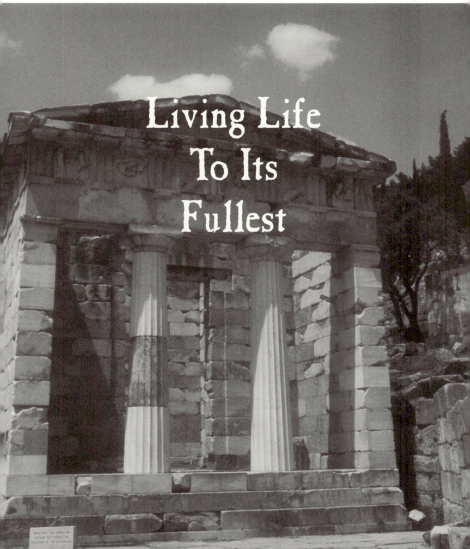

Living Life To Its Fullest

Follow your desire as long as you live; do not lessen the time of following desire, for the wasting of time is an abomination to the spirit.

Ptahhotpe (2350 B.C.)

Time is infinitely more precious than money, and there is nothing common between them. You cannot accumulate time; you cannot borrow time; you can never tell how much time you have left in the Bank of Life. Time is life...

Israel Davidson

The average adult has only about 300 months left to live. Let us spend this time every bit as carefully as we would spend our very last 300 dollars.

G.W.F.

First I was dying to finish high school and start college.
And then I was dying to finish college and start working.
And then I was dying to marry and have children.
And then I was dying for my children to grow old enough so I could return to work.
And then I was dying to retire.
And now, I am dying...and suddenly realize I forgot to live.

Anonymous

Life is not lost by dying; **life is lost minute by minute**, day by dragging day, in all the thousand small uncaring ways.

Stephen Vincent Benét (1898–1943)

Live all you can; it's a mistake not to. It doesn't so much matter what you do in particular, so long as you have your life. If you haven't had that, what have you had?

Henry James (1843–1916)

Resolved: To live with all my might while I do live, and as I shall wish I had done ten thousand ages hence.

Jonathan Edwards (1703–58)

As life is action and passion, it is required of man that he should share the passion and action of his time, at peril of being judged not to have lived.

Oliver Wendell Holmes, Jr. (1841–1935)

The follies which a person regrets most in his life are those he didn't commit when he had the opportunity.

Helen Rowland (1876–1950)

He who hesitates is a damned fool.

Mae West (1892–1980)

Momma always told me not to look into the eyes of the sun—but, momma, that's where the fun is!

Bruce Springsteen, <u>Blinded By The Light</u>

Water which is too pure has no fish.

Ts' ai Ken T'an

If your morals make you dreary, depend upon it they are wrong.

Robert Louis Stevenson (1850–94)

If I had my life to live over again, I'd try to make more mistakes next time...I would relax. I'd be sillier than I have been on this trip. I would climb more mountains, swim more rivers and watch more sunsets. I would have more actual troubles and less imaginary ones. Oh, I've had my moments, and if I had to do it over again, I'd have more of them. In fact, **I'd try to have nothing else**, just moments, one after another...I would pick more daisies.

Nadine Stair (at age 89)

There was a wise man in the Easata whose constant prayer was that he might see today with the eyes of tomorrow.

Alfred Mercier

Imagine returning to the misty past from the distant future when you're 80. Savor and embrace life **now** as you would. . .

G.W.F.

A person will be called to account on Judgment Day for every permissible thing he might have enjoyed but did not.

The Talmud

The most wasted of all days is that during which one has not laughed.

Sebastian Chamfort (1741–94)

The 11th commandment: Thou shalt be happy.

Author Unknown

On the whole, I am on the side of the unregenerate who affirm the worth of life as an end in itself, as against the saints who deny it.

Oliver Wendell Homes, Jr. (1841–1935)

Maybe you are here on earth to learn that life is what you make it, and it's to be enjoyed.

Dick Sutphen

The great opportunity is where you are. Do not despise your own place and hour. Every place is under the stars, every place is the center of the world.

John Burroughs (1837–1921)

Life is a great and wondrous mystery, and the only thing we know that we have for sure is what is right here right now. **Don't miss it.**

Leo Buscaglia

The invariable mark of wisdom is to see the miraculous in the common.

Ralph Waldo Emerson (1803–82)

Don't wait for extraordinary opportunities. Seize common occasions and make them great.

Orison Swett Marden

Keep in mind this daily notion: There **are** no ordinary moments.

Dan Millman, adapted

The art of being happy lies in the power of extracting happiness from common things.

Henry Ward Beecher (1813–87)

The moment one gives close attention to anything, even a blade of grass, it becomes a mysterious, awesome, indescribably magnificent world in itself.

Henry Miller (1891–1980)

The world is full of wonders and miracles but man takes his little hand and covers his eyes and sees nothing.

Israel Baal Shem

We take for granted the miraculous dance of creation, but the truly enlightened continuously see it as if for the first time.

Wes "Scoop" Nisker, adapted

I have often thought it would be a blessing if each human being were stricken blind and deaf for a few days during his early adult life. Darkness would make him more appreciative of sight; silence would teach him the joys of sound.

Helen Keller (1880–1968)

I should like to enjoy this summer flower by flower, as if it were to be the last one for me.

Andrè Gide (1869–1951)

Don't hurry. Don't worry. You're only here on a short visit, so don't forget to stop and smell the flowers.

Walter Hagan (1892–1969)

Take time to marvel at the wonders of life.

G.W.F.

Is this the little girl I carried; is this the little boy at play? I don't remember growing older...when did they? When did she grow to be a beauty; when did he grow to be so tall? Wasn't it yesterday when they were small? Sunrise, sunset, sunrise, sunset... quickly flow the days.

Fiddler on the Roof

You better take a fool's advice—take care of your own; 'cause one day they're here, next day they're gone.

Don Henley, New York Minute

All the wonderful things in life are so simple that one is not aware of their wonder until they are beyond touch. Never have I felt the wonder and beauty and joy of life so keenly as now in my grief that Johnny is not here to enjoy them. Today, when I see parents impatient or tired or bored with their children, I wish I could say to them, "but they are alive, think of the wonder of that! They may be a care and a burden, but think, they are alive! You can touch them— what a miracle!"

Frances Gunther

Teach your children to remind you, "But, Daddy, I'm only going to be young once!"

G.W.F.

The years race by in furious procession, making each hour a priceless possession.

Author Unknown

Savor the smiles and laughter of your children—there is **nothing** more important.

G.W.F.

Cherish your yesterdays; dream your tomorrows; but live your todays!

Author Unknown

There will come a day when you'd trade all of your tomorrows for a single yesterday. Enjoy these "yesterdays" fully.

G.W.F.

That man is a success who has lived well, laughed often and loved much.

Robert Louis Stevenson (1850–94)

Romancing

The

Present

Focus on today. Tomorrow is but a fantasy; yesterday is but a memory. **Today is the only reality.**

G.W.F.

The secret of health for both mind and body is not to mourn for the past, nor to worry about the future, but to live the present moment wisely and earnestly.

Buddha (563–483 B.C.)

A magic perspective: If you can bring up the drawbridges on yesterday and tomorrow in your mind, and **restrict yourself to today**...your cares will evaporate and your joys will skyrocket.

G.W.F.

Enjoy each moment. Appreciate what is. Be completely **here** and **now**. That is where eternity is found.

Peter McWilliams (sans John-Roger)

I don't know what tomorrow will bring— except old age and death—but I do know that I do have today, one absolutely glorious day that I will savor and make the most of as if it were my last one...because it may be!

G.W.F (1946—1995?)

You don't get to choose how you're going to die. Or when. You can only decide how you're going to live. **Now**.

Joan Baez

And thou wilt give thyself relief if thou doest every act of thy life as if it were the last.

Marcus Aurelius (120–180 B.C.)

These **are** the good old days.

Author Unknown

These are magic years...and therefore magic days...and therefore magic moments.

G.W.F.

Life is nothing but a series of moments. Start living the moments and the years will take care of themselves.

G.W.F.

We don't remember days; we remember moments.

Author Unknown

In **every moment**, the quality of your life is on the line. In each, you are either fully alive or relatively dead.

Dan Millman

Life is short. Be swift to love! Make haste to be kind!

Henri F. Amiel (1821–81)

Every moment is a golden one for him who has the vision to recognize it as such.

Henry Miller (1891–1980)

On Arturo Toscanini's eightieth birthday, someone asked his son, Walter, what his father ranked as his most important achievement. The son replied, "For him there can be no such thing. **Whatever he happens to be doing at the moment is the biggest thing in his life**—whether it is conducting a symphony or peeling an orange."

Ardis Whitman

Wherever you are, be there.

Author Unknown

You're searching, Joe, for things that don't exist; I mean beginnings. Ends and beginnings—there are no such things. There are only middles.

Robert Frost (1874–1963)

The little things? The little moments? They aren't little.

Jon Kabat-Zinn

All the gold in the world cannot buy a dying man one more breath—so what does that make today worth?!

Og Mandino, adapted

This is the first and the only time in the history of the entire world that today will happen. Live it with a vengeance.

G.W.F.

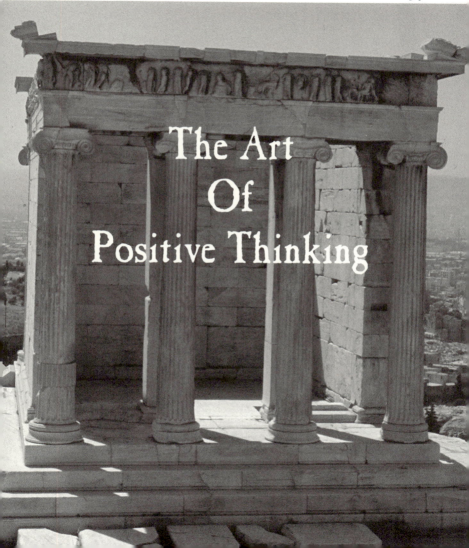

The Art
Of
Positive Thinking

The greatest discovery of my generation is that a human being can alter his life by altering his attitude of mind.

William James (1842–1910)

Our self image and our habits tend to go together. Change one and you will automatically change the other.

Dr. Maxwell Maltz

There is a basic law that **like attracts like**. Negative thinking definitely attracts negative results. Conversely, if a person habitually thinks optimistically and hopefully, his positive thinking sets in motion creative forces—and success instead of eluding him flows toward him.

Norman Vincent Peale, adapted

The world is what we think it is. **If we can change our thoughts, we can change the world.**

H. M. Tomlinson

Associate reverently, and as much as you can, with your loftiest thoughts.

Henry David Thoreau (1817–62)

By your thoughts you are daily, even hourly, building your life; you are carving your destiny.

Ruth Barrick Golden

Life does not consist mainly, or even large-ly, of facts and happenings. It consists main-ly of the storm of thoughts that are forever blowing through one's mind.

Mark Twain (1835–1910)

Your living is determined not so much by what life brings you as by the attitude you bring to life; not so much by what happens to you as by the way your mind looks at what happens.

Author Unknown

Every life has its dark and cheerful hours. Happiness comes from choosing which to remember.

Anonymous

The mind is like a river; upon its waters thoughts float through in a constant procession every conscious moment. You stand on a bridge over it and can stop and turn back any thought that comes along. The art of contentment is to **let no thought pass that is going to disturb you**.

Frank Crane, adapted

The art of being wise is the art of knowing what to overlook.

William James (1842–1910)

Nobody has the right to wreck your day, let alone your life. And guess what? Nobody does, you do. . .

G.W.F.

To be wronged is nothing unless you continue to remember it.

Confucius (551–479 B.C.)

He who harbors a slight will miss the haven of happiness.

Author Unknown

It is not possible for the human mind to hold both a positive and negative thought at the same time.

Lily Tomlin, adapted

Every tomorrow has two handles. You can take hold of the handle of anxiety or the handle of enthusiasm. **Upon your choice so will be the day.**

Author Unknown

We act as though comfort and luxury were the chief requirements of life, when all that we need to make us really happy is something to be enthusiastic about.

Charles Kingsley (1819–75)

One man has enthusiasm for 30 minutes, another for 30 days, but it is the man who has it for 30 years who makes a success of his life.

Edward B. Butler (1612–80)

A man can succeed at almost anything for which he has unlimited enthusiasm.

Charles Schwab

When a man dies, if he can pass enthusiasm along to his children, he has left them an estate of incalculable value.

Thomas Edison (1847–1931)

Given the three thousand million years of **chance occurrences** leading up to the chance encounter of one egg and one sperm that leads to the one cell that becomes you or me...the mere fact of existing should keep us all frozen in a **contented dazzlement of surprise**.

Opus, Outland

Start off by recognizing that everything is relative—you could have been a misspent sperm, a mayfly with a typical lifespan of several hours, or even a Frenchman.

Anonymous

Let not your mind run on what you lack as much as on what you have already. Of the things you have, select the best; and then reflect how eagerly they would have been sought if you did not have them.

Marcus Aurelius (120–180 A.D.)

If the good Lord took me tomorrow, I have already been luckier than any man has a right to be. Anything else is pure gravy.

G.W.F.

There is no one luckier than he who thinks himself so.

German Proverb

There's a "magic switch" inside all of us which can transform the worst to the best (or the best to the worst). It should be everyone's ultimate goal to discover and master this mechanism.

G.W.F.

The mind is its own place, and in itself can make a heaven of hell, or a hell of heaven.

John Milton (1608–74)

Only when we can love hell will we find heaven.

Anonymous

Learn to wish that everything should come to pass exactly as it does.

Epictetus (60–110 A.D.)

The highest possible stage in moral culture is when we recognize that we ought to control our thoughts.

Charles Darwin (1809–82)

For a man to conquer himself is the first and noblest of all victories.

Plato (427–347 B.C.)

Nothing is good or bad but that our thinking makes it so.

Shakespeare (1564–1616)

Two men look out through the same bars; one sees the mud and one the stars.

Frederick Langbridge (1849–1923)

We do not see things as **they** are. We see them as **we** are.

The Talmud

Life is but a mirror; it reflects back what you are.

G.W.F.

I have found that if you love life, life will love you back.

Arthur Rubenstein (1887–1982)

We have but one life—whether we spend it laughing or weeping.

Author Unknown

What a wonderful life I've had! I only wish I'd realized it sooner.

Colette (1873–1954)

This is the best day the world has ever seen. Tomorrow will be better.

R. A. Campbell

Realizing One's Potential

When you get to the Great Grandstand in the sky and look down on this Game of Life, you will come to realize: **there were no limits...!**

G.W.F.

If you can dream it, you can do it.

Walt Disney (1901–66)

There is a giant asleep within every man. When the giant awakes, miracles happen.

Frederick Faust

I am free to be what I want to be and to do what I want to do.

Jonathan Livingston Seagull

Nothing in the world can take the place of persistence. Talent will not; nothing is more common than unsuccessful men with talent. Genius will not; unrewarded genius is almost a proverb. Education will not; the world is full of educated failures. Persistence and determination alone are omnipotent.

Calvin Coolidge (1872–1933)

Do what you can, with what you have, where you are.

Theodore Roosevelt (1858–1919)

I am only one, but I am one. I cannot do everything; but I will not let what I cannot do interfere with what I can do.

Edward Everette Hale (1822–1909)

Do little things in an extraordinary way. You must not let your life run in the ordinary way; do something that nobody else has done, something that will dazzle the world. Show that God's creative principle works in you. Never mind the past. Have the unflinching determination to move on your path unhampered by limiting thoughts of past errors.

Paramahansa Yogananda

You've got to love like you'll never get hurt. You've got to dance like there's nobody watching. You've got to come from the heart if you want it to work.

Susanna Clarke

All the wonders you seek are within yourself.

Sir Thomas Brown (1605–82)

Oz never did give nothin' to the Tin Man that he didn't already have.

America, <u>Tin Man</u>

Within you right now is the power to do things you never dreamed possible. This power becomes available to you just as soon as you can **change your beliefs**.

Dr. Maxwell Maltz

Believe that you have it, and you have it.

Latin Proverb

So oftentimes it happens that we live our lives in chains and we never even know we have the key.

Eagles, Already Gone

It is very dangerous to go into eternity with possibilities which one has oneself prevented from becoming realities. A possibility is a thing from God. One must follow it.

Sören Kierkegaard (1813–55)

Most people go to their graves with their songs still unsung.

Oliver Wendell Holmes, adapted

Death is not the greatest loss in life. The greatest loss is what dies inside of us while we live.

Norman Cousins (1915–90)

Do not let time pass without accomplishing something. Otherwise you will regret it when your hair turns gray.

Yue Fei

One must have the adventurous daring to accept oneself as a bundle of possibilities and undertake the most interesting game in the world—making the most of one's best.

Harry Emerson Fosdick (1878–1969)

Make the most of yourself, for that is all there is of you.

Ralph Waldo Emerson (1803–82)

Regret for the things we did can be tempered by time; it is regret for the things we did not do that is inconsolable.

Sidney J. Harris

What keeps you from believing that the universe is yours? Reach out, embrace it. I say "the sky's the limit!" So get your bag, get your stuff, and head for the stars...I'll meet you out there.

Maura Beatty

In Search
Of
Happiness

Life is a paradise for those who love many things with a passion.

Leo Buscaglia

If you observe a really happy man, you will find him building a boat, writing a symphony, educating his son, growing double dahlias or looking for dinosaur eggs in the Gobi Desert. He will not be searching for happiness as if it were a collar button that had rolled under the radiator, striving for it as a goal in itself. He will have become aware that he is happy in the course of **living life twenty-four crowded hours of each day**.

W. Beran Wolfe (1900–35)

My opinion is that you never find happiness until you stop looking for it.

Chuang Tzu (5th–6th century B.C.)

In those moments when we forget ourselves—not thinking, "Am I happy?", but completely oblivious to our little ego—we spend a brief but beautiful holiday in heaven.

Eknath Easwaran

Why aren't you happy? It's because ninety-nine percent of everything you do, and think, and say, is for yourself.

Wu Wei Wu

To be happy is easy enough if we give ourselves, forgive others, and live with thanksgiving. No self-centered person, no ungrateful soul can ever be happy, much less make anyone else happy. Life is giving, not getting.

Joseph Fort Newton

If one only wished to be happy, this could be easily accomplished; but we wish to be happier than other people, and this is always difficult, for we believe others to be happier than they are.

Montesquieu (1688–1755)

The Law of Relativity: it is not so much what **oneself** has, or does not have, that concerns most people—it is what the **other person** has that ends up bothering us.

G.W.F.

If there were in the world today any large number of people who desired their own happiness more than they desired the unhappiness of others, we could have a paradise in a few years.

Bertrand Russell (1872–1970)

There are two things to aim at in life: first, to get what you want and, after that, to enjoy it. Only the wisest of mankind achieve the second.

Logan Pearsall Smith (1865–1946)

Who seeks more than he has hinders himself from enjoying what he has.

Solomon Ibn Gabirol (1021–58)

There is often less danger in the things we fear than in the things we desire.

John Churton Collins

The secret of contentment is knowing how to enjoy what you have, and to be able to lose all desire for things beyond your reach.

Lin Yutang

Never try to teach a pig to sing. It wastes your time and it just annoys the pig.

Author Unknown

It is the chiefest point of happiness that a man is willing to be what he is.

Desiderius Erasmus (1466–1536)

The secret of happiness is not in getting what you like, but in liking what you get.

James M. Barrie (1860–1937), adapted

I have noticed that folks are generally about as happy as they make up their minds to be.

Abraham Lincoln (1809–65)

Happiness is a present attitude—not a future condition.

Hugh Prather

Remember happiness doesn't depend upon who you are or what you have; it depends solely upon **what you think**.

Dale Carnegie (1888–1955)

The fountain of content must spring up in the mind, and he who has so little knowledge of human nature as to seek happiness **by changing anything but his own disposition** will waste his life in fruitless efforts and multiply the grief which he purposes to remove.

Samuel Johnson (1709–84)

A man's felicity consists not in the outward and visible blessings of fortune, but in the inward and unseen perfections and riches of the mind.

Anacharsis (c. 600 B.C.)

There is no value in life except what you choose to place upon it and no happiness in any place except what you bring to it yourself.

Henry David Thoreau (1817–62)

If you cannot be happy **here** and **now**, you never will be.

Taisen Peshimaru, adapted

Though we travel the world over to find the beautiful, we must carry it with us or we find it not.

Ralph Waldo Emerson (1803–82)

Wherever you go, there you are.

Author Unknown

Paradise is where I am.

Voltaire (1694–1778)

When we cannot find contentment in ourselves, it is useless to seek it elsewhere.

Francois Rochefoucauld (1613–80)

I am never bored anywhere; being bored is an insult to oneself.

Jules Renard

Happiness is not a state to arrive at, but a manner of traveling.

Samuel Johnson (1709–84)

The real secret of happiness is simply this: to be willing to live and let live, and to know very clearly in one's own mind that **the unpardonable sin is to be an unpleasant person**.

Galen Starr Ross

That person lives in hell who gets what he desires too soon. Happiness will be meaningless if it robs him of his desire. Heaven is a country through which we are permitted to search eagerly and with hope for what we want.

Thomas Dreier

To be without some of the things you want is an indispensible part of happiness.

Bertrand Russell (1872–1970)

Happiness is a way station between too little and too much.

Channing Pollock (1880–1946)

Happiness is found in the golden middle of two extremes.

Aristotle (384–322 B.C.)

Nothing in excess.

Temple at Delphi, Greece

There is no happiness where there is no wisdom.

Sophocles (496—06 B.C.)

The way to happiness: keep your heart free from hate, your mind from worry, live simply, expect little, give much.

Barney O'Lavin

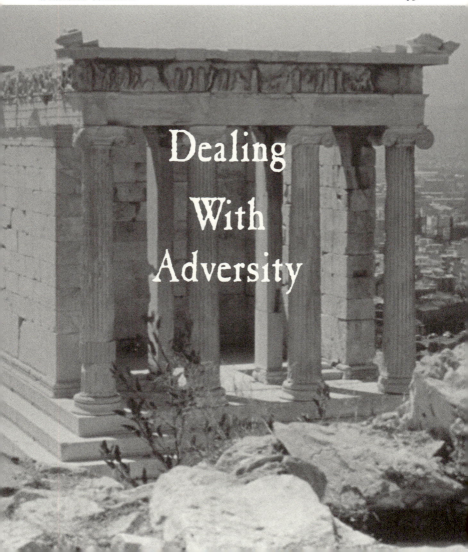

Dealing With Adversity

God allows us to experience the low points of life in order to teach us lessons we could not learn in any other way.

C. S. Lewis (1888–1965)

There is nothing the body suffers that the soul may not profit by.

George Meredith (1828–1909)

What doesn't kill me, makes me stronger.

Albert Camus (1913–60)

Many men owe the grandeur of their lives to their tremendous difficulties.

Charles H. Spurgeon (1834–92)

I thank God for my handicaps, for, through them, I have found myself, my work, and my God.

Helen Keller (1880–1968)

Looking back, we see with great clarity, and what once appeared as difficulties now reveal themselves as blessings.

Dan Millman

Old age, to the unlearned, is winter; to the learned, it is harvest time.

Yiddish Folk Saying

I'm looking forward to looking back on all this.

Sandra Knell

We could never learn to be brave and patient if there were only joy in the world.

Helen Keller (1880–1968)

One often learns more from ten days of agony than from ten years of contentment.

Merle Shain

The gem cannot be polished without friction, nor man perfected without trials.

Chinese Proverb

Failure is the greatest opportunity I have to know who I really am.

John Killinger

Make the most of every failure. Fall forward.

Author Unknown

Deferred joys purchased by sacrifice are always the sweetest.

Bishop Fulton Sheen (1895–1979)

Life is like a rollercoaster; the highs are meaningless but for the lows.

G.W.F.

Who has never tasted what is bitter does not know what is sweet.

German Proverb

There is a legend of a comfort-loving man who died and was borne to the other world where every wish was gratified. No effort, no struggle was required of him. He became bored and said "I can't stand this everlasting bliss any longer; I want to feel there are things I cannot have. I want to go to hell." The attendant replied: "And where do you think you are, sir?"

Harry O. Ritter

To appreciate heaven well, 'tis good for a man to have some fifteen minutes of hell.

Will Carleton

I cried because I had no shoes until I met a man who had no feet.

Persian saying

It is not what you have lost, but what you have left that counts.

Harold Russell

If you can't be thankful for what you receive, be thankful for what you escape.

Author Unknown

I don't want the cheese; I just want to get out of the trap.

Spanish Proverb

Take a mental walk through the cancer wards, the insane asylums, the homeless ghettoes, the children's hospitals...and re-ask yourself what is bothering you.

G.W.F.

But for the grace of God, I could be a blind, crippled beggar in the streets of Calcutta.

G.W.F.

If all our misfortunes were laid in one common heap whence everyone must take an equal portion, most people would be contented to take their own and depart.

Socrates (469–399 B.C.)

How dare you waste your life in self-pity. **Billions** of people gratefully would trade places with you!

G.W.F.

Happiness is not the absence of conflict, but the ability to cope with it.

Author Unknown

Life is mostly froth and bubble,
Two things stand like stone,
Kindness in another's trouble,
Courage in your own.

Adam Lindsay Gordon (1833—70)

Pain is inevitable. Suffering is optional.

Anonymous

Pain is simply the difference between what is and what I want it to be.

Spencer Johnson

For peace of mind, resign as general manager of the universe.

Larry Eisenberg

Beware of anxiety. Next to sin, there is nothing that so troubles the mind, strains the heart, distresses the soul, and confuses the judgment.

William Ullathorne

Drag your thoughts away from your troubles—by the ear, by the heels, or any other way you can manage it. It's the healthiest thing a body can do.

Mark Twain (1835–1910)

Happy is the man who has broken the chains which hurt the mind, and has **given up worrying once and for all.**

Ovid (43 B.C.–17 A.D.)

Worry does not empty tomorrow of its sorrow; it empties today of its joy.

Author Unknown

One hour of worry is one hour of hell.

James Dodd

When I look back on all these worries I remember the story of the old man who said on his deathbed that he had had a lot of trouble in his life, most of which never happened.

Winston Churchill (1874–1965)

How much pain the evils have cost us that never happened!

Thomas Jefferson (1743–1826)

Beware of desperate steps; the darkest day, lived till tomorrow, will have passed away.

William Cowper (1731–1800)

Keep cool; it will all be over 100 years hence.

Ralph Waldo Emerson (1803–82)

Life is too important to be taken seriously.

Oscar Wilde (1854–1900)

Rule #1—Don't sweat the small stuff.
Rule #2—It's almost all small stuff.

Robert S. Eliot, adapted

I saw somebody peeing in Jermyn Street the other day. I thought, is this the end of civilization as we know it? Or is it simply somebody peeing in Jermyn Street?

Alan Bennett

Today the greens are greener, the clouds are puffier, **the things that are important are more important**, and the things that aren't have gone way down.

A man who escaped death

No one will ever get out of this world alive. Resolve therefore to maintain a reasonable perspective and sense of values.

Lloyd Shearer

I realize now how precious each day is.

The late coach Jim Valvano

Once you have experienced the seriousness of your loss you will be able to experience the wonder of being alive.

Robert Veninga

Life is long if it is full.

Seneca (4 B.C.–65 A.D.)

That it will never come again is what makes life so sweet.

Emily Dickinson (1830–86)

Life...I absolutely love it and can't get enough of it!

G.W.F. (proclaimed after the death of a loved one)

The confrontation with death...makes everything look so precious, so sacred, so beautiful that I feel more strongly than ever the impulse to live it, to embrace it, and to let myself be overwhelmed by it.

Abraham Maslow (1908–70)

Do not stand at my grave and weep.

I am not there. I do not sleep.

I am a thousand winds that blow.

I am the diamond glints on snow.

I am the sunlight on ripened grain.

I am the gentle autumn's rain.

Do not stand at my grave and cry.

I am not there. I did not die.

Author Unknown (In memory of Dad, G.W.F.)

To live in hearts we leave behind is not to die.

Thomas Campbell (1777—1844)

What we have done for ourselves alone, dies with us. What we have done for others and the world, remains and is immortal.

Robert Pine

Remember—nothing will happen that you and God can't handle together.

Author Unknown

One night I dreamed I was walking along the beach with the Lord, and across the sky flashed scenes from my life. For each scene I noticed two sets of footprints in the sand; one belonged to me, the other to the Lord. When the last scene of my life flashed before us, I looked back at the footprints in the sand. I noticed that many times along the path of my life, there was only one set of footprints. I also noticed that it happened at the very lowest and saddest times of my life. I questioned the Lord about it. "Lord, you said that once I decided to follow You, You would walk with me all the way. But I have noticed that during the most troublesome times of my life, there was only one set of footprints. I don't understand why in times when I needed You most, You would leave." The Lord replied, "My precious child. I would never leave you **during your times of trial and suffering**. When you see only one set of footprints, **it was then that I carried you**."

Author Unknown

No man is in true health who can not stand in the free air of heaven, with his feet on God's free turf, and thank his Creator for the simple luxury of physical existence.

T. W. Higginson

The mere absence of any major problems at the present should be a cause, in and of itself, for euphoria.

G.W.F.

There are "problems" and there are **real** problems. The vast majority of us don't have **real** problems. Our failure to distinguish between these two and appreciate the difference constitutes a colossal distortion of thinking—which has served effectively to destroy more lives than all wars and diseases combined.

G.W.F

To hate and to fear is to be psychologically ill. It is, in fact, the consuming illness of our time.

H. A. Overstreet

The human mind often seems addicted to "awfulizing" and having troubles, and as soon as any particular problem does get resolved we become obsessed with replacing it with another problem—real or imaginary.

G.W.F.

Man, like a bridge, was designed to carry the load of the moment, not the combined weight of a year all at once.

William A. Ward

Write down the real difficulties on the left side of a page, and the imaginary difficulties on the right side. Only the ones on the right are unconquerable.

Marilyn Grey

What do we **need** fear for anyway? Pay five bucks to see a horror movie—get scared—then get on with your life.

Maura Beatty

However mean your life is, meet it and live it; do not shun it and call it hard names. It is not so bad as you are. The fault-finder will find fault even in paradise. Love your life.

Henry David Thoreau (1817–62)

With all its sham, drudgery and broken dreams, **it is still a beautiful world**. Be cheerful. Strive to be happy.

Desiderata (1692)

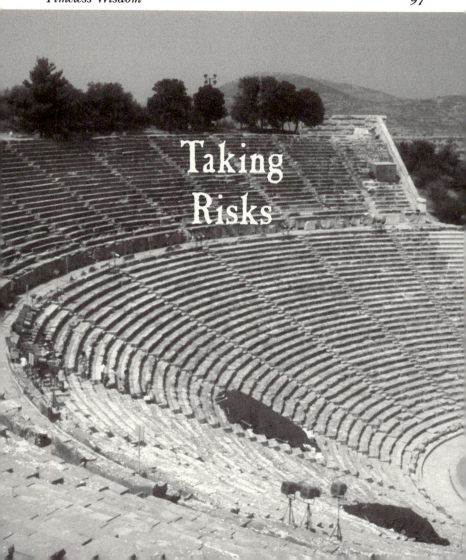

Taking
Risks

Life is either a daring adventure—or it is nothing.

Helen Keller (1880–1968)

So often life is every bit as good, if not better, than the wonderful make-believe movies we love to watch. It has all the same joy and sorrow, mystery and surprise, adventure and excitement, and love and emotion—except it's real. Live your life as if it were a great movie—complete with the happy ending.

G.W.F.

All the world's a stage, and you're the star!

Shakespeare (1564–1616), adapted

You know, we can't get out of life alive!
We can either die in the bleachers or die
on the field. We might as well come down
on the field and **go for it**!

Les Brown

Why wait? Life is not a dress rehearsal.
Quit practicing what you're going to do,
and just do it. In one bold stroke you can
transform today.

Marilyn Grey

We are always getting ready to live, but
never living.

Ralph Waldo Emerson (1803–82)

Don't let the fear of striking out hold you back.

Babe Ruth (1895–1948)
[Ruth held the all-time record for home runs
...and strikeouts!]

No man ever became great except through many and great mistakes.

William Ewart Gladstone (1809–98)

Only those who dare to fail greatly can ever achieve greatly.

Robert F. Kennedy (1925–68)

Why not go out on a limb? Isn't that where the fruit is?

Frank Scully

Mistakes are part of the dues one pays for a full life.

Sophia Loren

To try is to risk failure. But risk must be taken, as the greatest hazard in life is to risk nothing. **The person who risks nothing, does nothing, has nothing, and is nothing.**

Author Unknown

If your life is free of failures, you're not taking enough risks.

Author Unknown

Statistically—100% of the shots you don't take, don't go in.

Wayne Gretzsky

Concern yourself not with stumbles of the past or future. Only a worm does not stumble.

Og Mandino

Far better it is to **dare mighty things**, to win glorious triumphs even though checkered by failures, than to rank with those poor spirits who neither enjoy nor suffer much because they live in the gray twilight that knows neither victory nor defeat.

Theodore Roosevelt (1858–1919)

There are some defeats more triumphant than victories.

Michel de Montaigne (1533–92)

Do not be too timid and squeamish about your actions. All life is an experiment.

Ralph Waldo Emerson (1803–82)

Every year that I live I am more convinced that the waste of life lies in the love we have not given, the powers we have not used, the selfish prudence which will risk nothing, and which, shirking pain, misses happiness as well.

John B. Tabb (1845—1909)

I know you're still afraid to rush into anything...there're just so many summers,
Babe, just so many springs...

Don Henley, <u>Last Worthless Evening</u>

If one advances confidently in the direc-
tion of his dreams, and endeavors to live
the life which he has imagined, he will
meet with a success unexpected in common hours.

Henry David Thoreau (1817–62)

What would you attempt to do if you knew
you could not fail?

Dr. Robert Schuller

Act as if it were impossible to fail.

Dorothea Brande

In a world where death is the hunter, my friend, **there is no time for regrets or doubts**.

Carlos Castaneda

Understanding
Ourselves
And Others

Were we fully to understand the reasons for other people's behavior, it would all make sense.

Sigmund Freud (1856–1939), adapted

How to gain, how to keep, how to recover happiness, is in fact for most people at all times the secret motive for all they do and all they are willing to endure.

William James (1842–1910)

From his cradle to his grave a man never does a single thing which has any first and foremost object but one—to secure peace of mind, spiritual comfort, for himself.

Mark Twain (1835–1910)

No man consciously chooses evil because it is evil; he only mistakes it for happiness and the good that he seeks.

Mary Wollstonecraft Shelley (1797–1851), adapted

What do you call love, hate, charity, revenge, humanity, magnanimity, forgiveness? Different results of the one Master Impulse: The necessity of securing one's self-approval.

Mark Twain (1835–1910)

The deepest principle of human nature is the craving to be appreciated.

William James (1842–1910)

Men are not against you; they are merely for themselves.

Gene Fowler

Half of the harm that is done in this world is due to people who want to feel important...**they do not mean to do harm**...they are absorbed in an endless struggle to think well of themselves.

T. S. Eliot (1888–1965)

I used to love to make you cry; it made me feel like a man inside...

Frankie Valli and The Four Seasons,
Working My Way Back To You

Deep down inside, underneath it all, we're all running scared.

G.W.F.

Be kind, for everyone you meet is fighting a hard battle.

Plato (427–347 B.C.)

If we could read the secret history of our enemies, we would find in each man's life a sorrow and a suffering enough to disarm all hostility.

Henry Wadsworth Longfellow (1807–82)

Rest assured that, generally speaking, others are acting in exactly the same manner that you would under exactly the same circumstances...Hence, be kind, understanding, empathetic, non-judgmental and forgiving.

G.W.F.

Whatever you may be sure of, be sure of this—that you are dreadfully like other people.

James Russell Lowell (1819–91)

When you try to understand everything, you will not understand anything. The best way is to understand yourself, and then you will understand everything.

Shunryu Suzuki (1870–1966)

I am the entire human race compacted together. I have found that there is no ingredient of the race which I do not possess in either a small way or a large way.

Mark Twain (1835–1910)

To know others you do not have to go and knock on four billion separate doors. Once you have seen your real Self, you have seen the Self in all.

Eknath Easwaran

I observe myself and I come to know others.

Lao-Tzu (604–531 B.C.)

Treat people as if they were what they ought to be and you help them to become what they are capable of being.

Johann Wolfgang von Goethe (1749–1832)

To make anyone believe himself good is to make him, almost in spite of self, to become so.

Charlotte M. Yonge

Really great men have a curious feeling that the greatness is not in them, but through them. And they see something divine in every other man.

John Ruskin (1819–1900)

Rare is the person who can weigh the faults of others without putting his thumb on the scales.

Byron J. Langenfeld

When you see a good man, think of emulating him; when you see a bad man, **examine your heart**.

Chinese Proverb

The only devils in the world are those running in our own hearts. That is where the battle should be fought.

Mahatma Gandhi (1869–1948)

We have seen the enemy and it is us.

Pogo

We are our own devils; we drive ourselves out of our Edens.

Johann Wolfgang von Goethe (1749–1832)

Be not angry that you cannot make others as you wish them to be since you cannot make yourself as you wish to be.

Thomas à Kempis (1380–1471)

Resolve to be tender with the young, compassionate with the aged, sympathetic with the striving, and tolerant with the weak and the wrong. Sometime in life you will have been all of these.

Lloyd Shearer

Oh, great Father, never let me judge another man until I have walked in his moccasins for two weeks.

Indian Prayer

If you judge people, you have no time to love them.

Mother Teresa

God himself, sir, does not propose to judge a man until the end of his days.

Samuel Johnson (1709–84)

How can we venture to judge others when we know so well how ill-equipped they are for judging us.

Comtesse Diane

Judge not, that ye not be judged.

Jesus

When you judge someone you don't define them, you define yourself.

Dr. Wayne Dyer

I tell you one thing, if you want peace of mind, do not find fault with others.

Sri Sarada Devi (1836–86)

The only people to get even with are those who helped you.

Author Unknown

One word frees us all of the weight and pain of life. That word is Love.

Sophocles (496–406 B.C.)

If you do not learn how to love, **everywhere you go you are going to suffer**.

Eknath Easwaran

So when the shoe fits, the foot is forgotten; when the belt fits, the belly is forgotten; when the heart is right, "for" and "against" are forgotten.

Thomas Merton (1915–68)

Out beyond the ideas of right-doing and wrong-doing is a field—I'll meet you there.

Jalal al-Din al-Rumi (1207–73)

I think the greatest thing in the world is to believe in people.

John Galsworthy (1867–1933)

In spite of everything, I still believe that people are really good at heart.

Anne Frank (1929–45)

Loving
And Serving
Others

Hatred does not cease through hatred at any time. Hatred ceases through love. **This is an unalterable law.**

The Buddha (563–483 B.C.)

Love and you shall be loved. All love is mathematically just, as much as the two sides of an algebraic equation.

Ralph Waldo Emerson (1803–82)

To forgive is the highest, most beautiful form of love. In return, you will receive untold peace and happiness.

Robert Muller

Forgiving means to pardon the unpardonable and loving means to love the unlovable. Or it is no virtue at all.

G. K. Chesterton (1874–1936)

The weak can never forgive. Forgiveness is the attribute of the strong.

Mahatma Gandhi (1869–1948)

He who cannot forgive others destroys the bridge over which he himself must pass.

George Herbert (1593–1633)

Self-love is not only necessary and good, it is a prerequisite for loving others.

Rollo May

The person who pursues revenge should dig two graves.

Author Unknown

Those who are at war with others are not at peace with themselves.

William Hazlitt (1778–1830)

Never, ever engage in envy or hatred—it is a mental cancer that will only destroy oneself.

G.W.F.

He who angers you, conquers you.

Elizabeth Kenny (1886–1952)

Those whom God wishes to destroy he first makes angry.

Euripides (484–406 B.C.), adapted

Beginning today, treat everyone you meet as if they were going to be dead by midnight. Extend to them all the care, kindness, and understanding you can muster, and do with no thought of any reward. **Your life will never be the same again**.

Og Mandino

It is only upon death and at the funeral that we rejoice in the glory of each person's life and capture the true spirit of love... Let every day be doomsday!

G.W.F.

The way to love anything is to realize that it might be lost.

G. K. Chesterton (1874–1936)

If one were given five minutes warning before sudden death, five minutes to say what it had all meant to us, every telephone booth would be occupied by people trying to call up other people to stammer that they loved them.

Christopher Morley (1890–1957)

Call now.

G.W.F.

No man can live happily who regards himself alone, who turns everything to his own advantage. You must live for others if you wish to live for yourself.

Seneca (4 B.C.–65 A.D.)

It is one of the most beautiful compensations of life that no man can sincerely try to help another without helping himself.

Ralph Waldo Emerson (1803–82)

Down in their hearts, wise men know this truth: the only way to help yourself is to help others.

Elbert Hubbard (1856–1915)

I don't know what your destiny will be, but one thing I know: the only ones among you who will be truly happy are those who will have sought and found how to serve.

Albert Schweitzer (1875–1965)

It is uncomfortable doctrine which the true ethics whisper into my ear: you are happy, they say; therefore you are called upon to give much.

Albert Schweitzer (1875–1965)

We have no more right to consume happiness without producing it than to consume wealth without producing it.

George Bernard Shaw (1856–1950)

You have not lived a perfect day, unless you have done something for someone who will never be able to repay you.

Ruth Smeltzer

Unless we think of others and do something for them, we miss one of the greatest sources of happiness.

Ray Lyman Wilbur

Doing good is one of life's greatest highs.

G.W.F.

We make a living by what we get, we make a life by what we give.

Sir Winston Churchill (1874–1965)

He who receives a benefit should never forget it; he who bestows should never remember it.

Pierre Charron

This is the final test of a gentleman: his respect for those who can be of no possible service to him.

William Lyon Phelps

Act with kindness, but do not expect gratitude.

Confucius (551–479 B.C.)

Donate anonymously—that is the ultimate and true spirit of charity.

G.W.F.

If you want happiness for an hour—take a nap.

If you want happiness for a day—go fishing.

If you want happiness for a month—get married.

If you want happiness for a year—inherit a fortune.

If you want happiness for a lifetime—help others.

Chinese Proverb

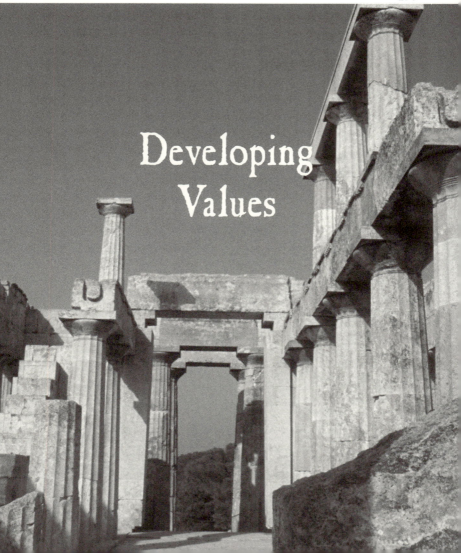

Developing Values

To love God truly, one must first love man. And if anyone tells you that he loves God and does not love his fellow man, you will know that he's lying.

Hassidic Saying

When you hear a man say, "I hate," adding the name of some race, nation, religion, or social class, you are dealing with a belated mind. That man may dress like a modern, ride in an automobile, listen over the radio, but his mind is properly dated about 1000 B.C.

Henry Emerson Fosdick (1878–1969)

Hatred toward any human being cannot exist in the same heart as love to God.

Dean William Inge (1860–1954)

He does not believe who does not live according to his belief.

Thomas Fuller (1608–61)

Men are all alike in their promises. It is only in their deeds that they differ.

Molière (1622–73)

If one is to do good one must do it in the minute particulars. General good is the plea of the hypocrite, the flatterer and the scoundrel.

William Blake (1757–1827)

He who is not liberal with what he has, deceives himself when he thinks he would be more liberal if he had more.

W. S. Plumer

If, after I depart this vale, you ever remember me and have thought to please my ghost, forgive some sinner and wink your eye at some homely girl.

H. L. Mencken (1880–1956)

Do little nice things for people to make this world a better place. Then do **BIG** things to make this world a better place.

G.W.F.

He who waits to do a great deal of good at once will never do anything.

Author Unknown

The road to Hell is paved with good intentions; the road to Heaven is paved with good deeds.

Author Unknown

I shall tell you a great secret, my friend. Do not wait for the last judgment; it takes place every day.

Albert Camus (1913–60)

When God measures a man, He puts the tape around the heart instead of the head.

Author Unknown

When it's all over, will you be able to look Him in the eye?

G.W.F.

In a community in which there is involuntary starvation every well-fed person is a thief.

Holbrook Jackson

Sell whatever thou hath, and give it to the poor, and thou shalt have treasure in heaven; and come, take up the cross, and follow me.

Two sources: a carpenter from Nazareth and a street-corner "crazy" in New York City

People in general are equally horrified at hearing the Christian religion doubted, and at seeing it practiced.

Samuel Butler (1835–1902)

Christianity might be a good thing if any-one ever tried it.

George Bernard Shaw (1856–1950)

If you are what you do, and then you don't, you aren't.

Robert Subby

We have committed the Golden Rule to memory. Let us now commit it to life.

Author Unknown

The world is my country; mankind is my brethren; **to do good is my religion.**

Thomas Paine (1737–1809)

Each man has a choice in life: he may approach it as a creator or a critic, a lover or a hater, a giver or a taker.

Author Unknown

We all end up on the giving or receiving side. As long as God allows I will gladly and gratefully choose the giving side.

G.W.F.

The test of thankfulness is not what you have to be thankful for, but whether anyone else has reason to be thankful that you are here.

Author Unknown

Life, to a large extent, is a "constant sum" game; generally you have benefited due to someone else's loss. The "rules of the game" are for the winners to give some of it back to the losers...

G.W.F.

You should never take more than you give in the Circle of Life.

Elton John, <u>Circle of Life</u>

Always do right. This will gratify some people, and astonish the rest.

Mark Twain (1835–1910)

There is never a wrong time to do the right thing.

Author Unknown

To see what is right and not do it is want of courage.

Confucius (551–479 B.C.)

The only thing necessary for the triumph of evil is for good men to do nothing.

Edmund Burke (1729–97)

Live so that when your children think of fairness, caring and integrity, they think of you.

H. Jackson Browne, Jr.

If you compare yourself with others you may become vain and bitter; for there will always be greater and lesser persons than yourself.

Desiderata (1692)

Pride leads to destruction, and arrogance to downfall.

Proverbs 16:18

If Christ was able to remain humble, perhaps the rest of us could also manage to do so.

G.W.F.

How great some men would be if they
were not arrogant.

Talmud

Nearly all men can stand adversity, but if
you want to test a man's character, give him
power.

Abraham Lincoln (1809–65)

A person is no longer great once he
thinks he is so.

G.W.F.

Great minds discuss ideas, average minds
discuss events, small minds discuss people.

Laurence J. Peter

The words of the tongue should have three gatekeepers:

- Is it true?

  - Is it kind?

    - Is it necessary?

Arab Proverb

Never say anything about others that you wouldn't want them to hear—because they probably will.

G.W.F.

What you say tells other people what you are.

Author Unknown

Remember, what you possess in the world will be found at the day of your death to belong to someone else, but what you are will be yours forever.

Henry Van Dyke

If you want to know how rich you really are, find out what would be left of you tomorrow if you should lose every dollar you own tonight.

William J. H. Boetcker

Do not care overly much for wealth or power or fame, or one day you will meet someone who cares for none of these things, and **you will realize how poor you have become**.

Rudyard Kipling (1865–1936)

Do you know what real poverty is? It is never having a big thought or a generous impulse.

Jerome P. Fleishman

It is the preoccupation with possession, more than anything else, that prevents man from living freely and nobly.

Bertrand Russell (1872–1970)

A man there was and they called him mad; the more he gave the more he had.

John Bunyan (1628–88)

They who give have all things; they who withhold have nothing.

Hindu Proverb

The sage does not accumulate for himself. The more he gives to others, the more he possesses of his own. The way of Heaven is to benefit others and not to injure.

Lao-Tzu (604–531 B.C.)

The bird of paradise alights only upon the hand that does not grasp.

John Berry

Superfluous wealth can buy superfluities only. Money is not required to buy one necessity of the soul.

Henry David Thoreau (1817–62)

What shall it profit a man, if he shall gain the whole world, and lose his own soul?

Mark 8:36

The Chinese tell of a man of Peiping who dreamed of gold, much gold, his heart's desire. He rose one day and when the sun was high he dressed in his finest garments and went to the crowded market place. He stepped directly to the booth of a gold dealer, snatched a bag full of gold coins, and walked calmly away. The officials who arrested him were puzzled: "Why did you rob the gold dealer in broad daylight?" they asked. "And in the presence of so many people?"

"I did not see any people," the man replied. **"I saw only gold**."

Louis Binstock

I once got a huge check. And the same day I got a huge hug and kiss from my child. The hug and kiss felt better.

G.W.F

True contentment depends not upon what we have; a tub was large enough for Diogenes, but a world was too little for Alexander.

Charles Caleb Colton (1780–1832)

Wisdom leads to tranquility; gold and silver to anxiety.

Solomon Ibn Gabirol (1021–58)

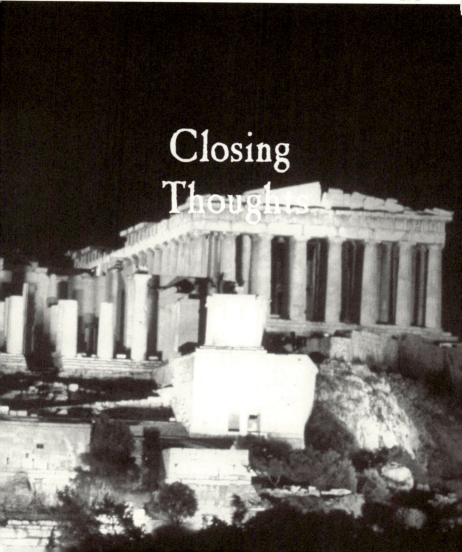

Closing Thoughts

What is bad to you, do not to others. That is the entire law; all the rest is commentary.

The Talmud

Just one great idea can completely revolutionize your life.

Earl Nightengale

Good thoughts are no better than good dreams if you don't follow through.

Ralph Waldo Emerson (1803–82)

If we do not change our daily lives, we cannot change the world.

Thich Nhat Hanh

"Your task...to build a better world," God said. I answered "How?...this world is such a large, vast place, and there's nothing I can do." But God in all his wisdom said, "**just build a better you**".

Author Unknown

Live every day as if it were your last. Treat everybody else as if he were you.

Author Unknown

Be such a man, and live such a life, that if every man were such as you, and every life a life like yours, this earth would be God's Paradise.

Phillips Brooks (1835–93)

On the Day of Judgment, we shall not be asked what we have read, but what we have done.

Thomas à Kempis (1380–1471)

Wisdom is knowing what to do next; virtue is doing it.

David Starr Jordan (1851–1931)

Whatever you can do, or dream you can, **begin it**. Boldness has genius, power and magic in it.

W. H. Murray

To change one's life:

- Start immediately,
  - Do it flamboyantly,
    - No exceptions!

William James (1842—1910)

To laugh often and much, to win the respect of intelligent people and the affection of children; to earn the appreciation of honest critics and endure the betrayal of false friends; to appreciate beauty; to find the best in others; to leave the world a bit better, whether by a healthy child, a garden patch or a redeemed social condition; to know even one life has breathed easier because you have lived. This is to have succeeded.

Ralph Waldo Emerson (1803–82)

There are three marks of a superior man: being virtuous, he is free from anxiety; being wise, he is free from perplexity; being brave, he is free from fear.

Confucius (551–479 B.C.)

If wisdom were offered me with the proviso that I should keep it shut up and refrain from declaring it, I should refuse. There's no delight in owning anything unshared.

Seneca (4 B.C.–65 A.D.)

Surprise and confound the world with your enthusiasm and optimism; **you know something they don't**.

G.W.F.